# READ ABOUT IT

## Activities for Teaching Basic Reading Skills
## Middle Grades

Imogene Forte

# Thank You

to Mary Catherine Mahoney
and to Elaine Raphael
editors
to Dennas Davis
cover designer
and especially to Mary Hamilton
artist and wordsmith

Library of Congress Catalog Card Number 82-80502
ISBN 0-86530-007-0

# These Adventures In Reading
## Belong To

_____

If you can catch the Unicorn
And mount it for a ride,
You'll find that hidden, secret worlds
Appear before your eyes.

You'll meet with gnomes and goblins,
Fauns and fairies, friends and foes.
No dreamy realm of fantasy
Is very far from home.

You'll walk the land of giants, those
In fearsome forests lie.
The Unicorn will take you there
And never leave your side.

So ride away the Unicorn
To know the world that was,
The world the way it is today,
Or what is yet to come.

Adventure lasts a lifetime if
You're willing to pursue
Each newly opened book to bring
The Unicorn to you!

# ABOUT THIS BOOK

READ ABOUT IT was written to provide interesting, fun-filled pages to help boys and girls achieve reading independence. The activities have been carefully designed to reinforce and extend vocabulary and comprehension skills. Easy-to-follow directions, fanciful fantasy-based themes, and the use of a controlled but not limited vocabulary encourage purposeful reading.

To simplify classroom or home use, the reproducible skills-based activity pages have been organized into two broad areas:

    I.  Word recognition and usage
        A.  Structural analysis
        B.  Word meaning
        C.  Word sensitivity

    II.  Independent reading skills
        A.  Comprehension
        B.  Work/study
        C.  Library and reference materials
        D.  Rate, accuracy, and appreciation

Each of the worksheets is designed to stand alone and to present one complete reading experience. They may be used to supplement and reinforce adopted textbooks and courses of study and are appropriate for use in either individual or group settings. For classroom use, teachers will want to review the skills as listed in the table of contents and plan the order and manner of presentation to meet student needs. In a home or other setting where the book is used individually, the pages will fall into a natural skills sequence and can be used most efficiently in the order presented.

The purposes of this collection of read-think-and-do pencil and paper activities, puzzles, games, and fun projects are to encourage kids to stretch their minds, develop their imaginations, and enjoy the thrill of successful personal reading.

Come, let's READ ABOUT IT!

Imogene Forte

# TABLE OF CONTENTS

**WORD RECOGNITION AND USAGE SKILLS** . . . . . . . . . . . . . . . . . . . . . . . . . . . . . . . . 11

Prefix Pyramids
    using prefixes . . . . . . . . . . . . . . . . . . . . . . . . . . . . . . . . . . . . . 13
Suffixes for the Sorcerer
    using suffixes . . . . . . . . . . . . . . . . . . . . . . . . . . . . . . . . . . . . . 14
The Mermaid's Tale
    recognizing contractions and possessives . . . . . . . . . . . . . . . . . . . . . . . . 15
A Short Letter
    recognizing and using abbreviations . . . . . . . . . . . . . . . . . . . . . . . . 16
What's the Weather?
    recognizing compound words . . . . . . . . . . . . . . . . . . . . . . . . 17
It's Not a Pretty Picture!
    using picture clues . . . . . . . . . . . . . . . . . . . . . . . . . . . . 18
Thrifty Timothy Thorngill
    using context clues . . . . . . . . . . . . . . . . . . . . . . . . . . . . 19
Scrambled Eggs
    classifying words . . . . . . . . . . . . . . . . . . . . . . . . . . . . . . 20
Tale of a Tacky Troll
    classifying words . . . . . . . . . . . . . . . . . . . . . . . . . . . . . . 21
Different Words, Different Story
    recognizing antonyms . . . . . . . . . . . . . . . . . . . . . . . . . . . 22
Mark the Homonym Trail
    recognizing homonyms . . . . . . . . . . . . . . . . . . . . . . . . . . 23
Test Your Word Knowledge
    recognizing synonyms and antonyms . . . . . . . . . . . . . . . . . . . . 24
The Incredible Math Machine
    using words in content areas . . . . . . . . . . . . . . . . . . . . . . . . 25
Pixie Power
    developing word meaning . . . . . . . . . . . . . . . . . . . . . . . . . 26
A Scary Story
    associating words with feelings . . . . . . . . . . . . . . . . . . . . . . 27
On Stage
    forming sensory impressions . . . . . . . . . . . . . . . . . . . . . . . . 28
Say What You Mean!
    interpreting idiomatic expressions . . . . . . . . . . . . . . . . . . . . . 29
Sentence Special
    interpreting sensations suggested by words . . . . . . . . . . . . . . . . 30
In the Mood
    interpreting moods . . . . . . . . . . . . . . . . . . . . . . . . . . . . . 31
A Word on Moods
    interpreting moods . . . . . . . . . . . . . . . . . . . . . . . . . . . . . 32
An Evil Ogre
    recognizing word relationships . . . . . . . . . . . . . . . . . . . . . . . 33
Werner and Victor
    recognizing word relationships . . . . . . . . . . . . . . . . . . . . . . . 34
Seven Children To Describe
    recognizing and using descriptive words . . . . . . . . . . . . . . . . . . 35
Midnight Madness
    recognizing and using descriptive words . . . . . . . . . . . . . . . . . . 36
Word-Ability Wizard
    developing word appreciation . . . . . . . . . . . . . . . . . . . . . . . . 37
With Words in Mind
    developing word appreciation . . . . . . . . . . . . . . . . . . . . . . . . 38
Words on the Line
    extending vocabulary . . . . . . . . . . . . . . . . . . . . . . . . . . . . 39

**INDEPENDENT READING SKILLS** . . . . . . . . . . . . . . . . . . . . . . . . . . . . . . . . . . 41

Up the Beanstalk
    reading for a specific purpose . . . . . . . . . . . . . . . . . . . . . . . . 43
The Knight's Journey
    finding the main idea . . . . . . . . . . . . . . . . . . . . . . . . . . . . 44
Goblins for Christmas
    reading to find details . . . . . . . . . . . . . . . . . . . . . . . . . . . 45
Number, Please
    reading to find details . . . . . . . . . . . . . . . . . . . . . . . . . . . 46
The Elixir of Invisibility
    reading to find details . . . . . . . . . . . . . . . . . . . . . . . . . . . 47

Detail Selection
    reading to find details . . . . . . . . . . . . . . . . . . . . . . . . . . . . . . . . . . . . . . . . . . .48
Ballow's Dilemma
    arranging ideas in sequence . . . . . . . . . . . . . . . . . . . . . . . . . . . . . . . . . . . . . . .49
How Does It End?
    arranging ideas in sequence . . . . . . . . . . . . . . . . . . . . . . . . . . . . . . . . . . . . . . .50
Fable Frames
    arranging events in sequence . . . . . . . . . . . . . . . . . . . . . . . . . . . . . . . . . . . . . .51
Bookshelf
    classifying material read . . . . . . . . . . . . . . . . . . . . . . . . . . . . . . . . . . . . . . . . . .52
Storm Warning
    summarizing . . . . . . . . . . . . . . . . . . . . . . . . . . . . . . . . . . . . . . . . . . . . . . . . . . .53
Let the Gnomes Know
    summarizing . . . . . . . . . . . . . . . . . . . . . . . . . . . . . . . . . . . . . . . . . . . . . . . . . . .54
What Next?
    drawing conclusions . . . . . . . . . . . . . . . . . . . . . . . . . . . . . . . . . . . . . . . . . . . . .55
How Famous Is Famous?
    questioning . . . . . . . . . . . . . . . . . . . . . . . . . . . . . . . . . . . . . . . . . . . . . . . . . . . .56
Tell It Your Way
    predicting outcomes . . . . . . . . . . . . . . . . . . . . . . . . . . . . . . . . . . . . . . . . . . . . .57
How Big Is This Big Deal?
    distinguishing between fact and opinion . . . . . . . . . . . . . . . . . . . . . . . . . . . . . .58
Careless Clara Clark
    determining cause and effect . . . . . . . . . . . . . . . . . . . . . . . . . . . . . . . . . . . . . .59
Character Portraits
    identifying character traits . . . . . . . . . . . . . . . . . . . . . . . . . . . . . . . . . . . . . . . .60
As You See It
    visualizing . . . . . . . . . . . . . . . . . . . . . . . . . . . . . . . . . . . . . . . . . . . . . . . . . . . .61
Organizing a Newsstand
    alphabetizing . . . . . . . . . . . . . . . . . . . . . . . . . . . . . . . . . . . . . . . . . . . . . . . . . .62
Author Under Investigation
    using multiple resources . . . . . . . . . . . . . . . . . . . . . . . . . . . . . . . . . . . . . . . . . .63
A Word or Two on the World
    using multiple resources . . . . . . . . . . . . . . . . . . . . . . . . . . . . . . . . . . . . . . . . . .64
Choose a Country
    using multiple resources . . . . . . . . . . . . . . . . . . . . . . . . . . . . . . . . . . . . . . . . . .65
The Humble Cook
    using the thesaurus . . . . . . . . . . . . . . . . . . . . . . . . . . . . . . . . . . . . . . . . . . . . .66
Finders Keepers
    using library materials . . . . . . . . . . . . . . . . . . . . . . . . . . . . . . . . . . . . . . . . . . .67
Library Lover's Law
    developing library appreciation . . . . . . . . . . . . . . . . . . . . . . . . . . . . . . . . . . . .68
Skimming the News
    using the newspaper . . . . . . . . . . . . . . . . . . . . . . . . . . . . . . . . . . . . . . . . . . . .69
Running Errands
    following written directions . . . . . . . . . . . . . . . . . . . . . . . . . . . . . . . . . . . . . . .70
Reading Project Plan
    using systematically organized materials . . . . . . . . . . . . . . . . . . . . . . . . . . . . .71
Weighing an Elephant
    using punctuation . . . . . . . . . . . . . . . . . . . . . . . . . . . . . . . . . . . . . . . . . . . . . .72
Outline Pin-Up
    taking notes from reading . . . . . . . . . . . . . . . . . . . . . . . . . . . . . . . . . . . . . . . .73
Ride the Unicorn!
    developing appreciation and independence . . . . . . . . . . . . . . . . . . . . . . . . . . . .74
Character Selection
    developing appreciation and independence . . . . . . . . . . . . . . . . . . . . . . . . . . . .75
Fairy Tale Favorite
    developing appreciation and independence . . . . . . . . . . . . . . . . . . . . . . . . . . . .76
Shelve It!
    developing appreciation and independence . . . . . . . . . . . . . . . . . . . . . . . . . . . .77
Good Books Belong Outdoors
    developing appreciation and independence . . . . . . . . . . . . . . . . . . . . . . . . . . . .78


ANSWER KEY . . . . . . . . . . . . . . . . . . . . . . . . . . . . . . . . . . . . . . . . . . . . . . . . . . . . . . .79

# WORD RECOGNITION AND USAGE
# SKILLS

*If you can catch the Unicorn*
*And mount it for a ride,*
*You'll find that hidden, secret worlds*
*Appear before your eyes.*

# PREFIX PYRAMIDS

Long ago in the Egyptian desert, the famous Pyramids of the Pharaohs were built.

You, too, can be a pyramid builder.

Add the prefix at the top of each empty pyramid shape to root words from the list below to build each prefix pyramid.

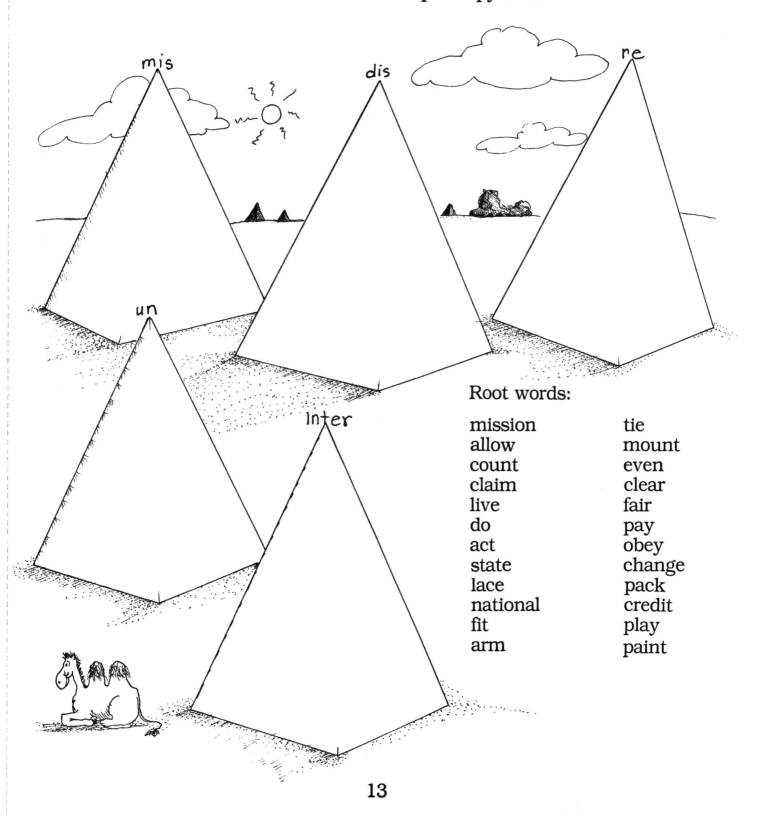

Root words:

| | |
|---|---|
| mission | tie |
| allow | mount |
| count | even |
| claim | clear |
| live | fair |
| do | pay |
| act | obey |
| state | change |
| lace | pack |
| national | credit |
| fit | play |
| arm | paint |

# SUFFIXES FOR THE SORCERER

This sorcerer is trying to make a name for himself by adding new words to the Sorcerer Society's Suffix Bag. Help him by dipping into the dragon's pool for words to add to the suffixes. Write them in their proper places on the bag to make new words.

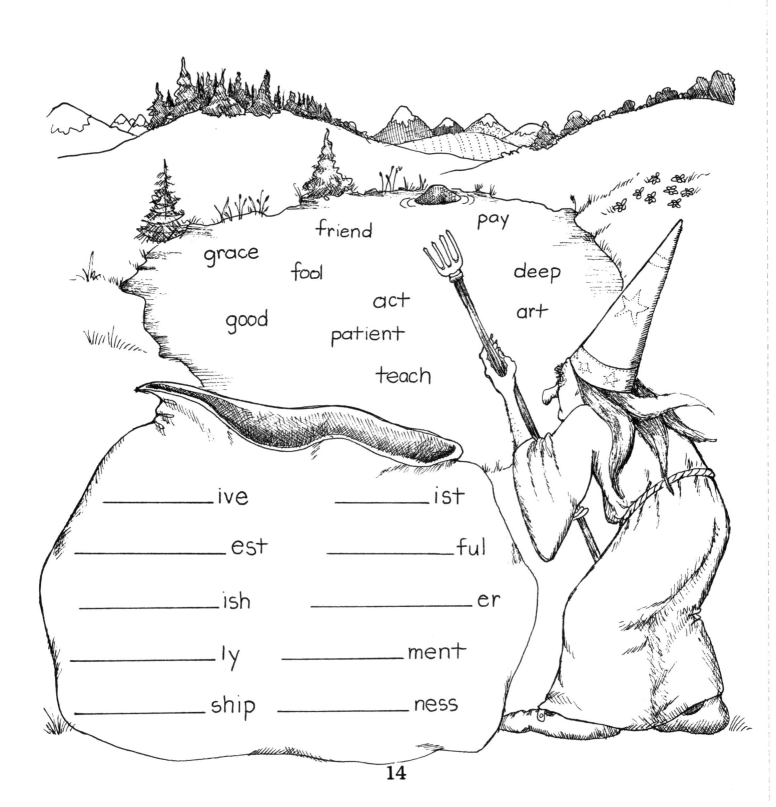

friend

pay

grace

fool

deep

act

art

good

patient

teach

_____ive          _____ist

_____est          _____ful

_____ish          _____er

_____ly           _____ment

_____ship         _____ness

# THE MERMAID'S TALE

Underline the phrase or phrases in each group which contain a contraction.

Circle the phrase or phrases in each group which contain an apostrophe to show possession.

1. The mermaid's fins
   She doesn't know
   The ocean's floor

2. The waves' roar
   They can't hear
   It wasn't safe

3. Shouldn't she go
   Her mother's party
   She'll know soon

4. The boat's sail
   I'm interested
   Here's another story

5. She'll tell me
   I'll never tell
   The sea's secrets

6. There's treasure
      somewhere
   They'll keep searching
   The diver's work

7. She didn't remember
   Her friend's message
   It's getting late

8. The sailor's question
   Merry's answer
   The tale's almost told

9. Here's the chest
   The gold's glitter
   You've guessed the
      secret

# A SHORT LETTER

Humberto the Traveling Magician wrote the letter below to his twin sister Herberta. Since Humberto had to carry all his belongings on his back, he kept only one small sheet of paper and a short, stubby pencil in his canvas backpack. He used all the abbreviations he could to make his letter short.

Herberta could read her brother's letter easily, but their elderly mother had trouble. Help the poor lady out by circling each abbreviation and writing the words it stands for in the correct blank at the bottom of the page.

Dear Herberta,

Tomorrow, Aug. 17, at 6:00 a.m., I leave for Prince Edward Is. in the Gulf of St. Lawrence, just n. of Nova Scotia. I'm joining Dr. Hamilton and Mr. Snowden for a fishing trip on their 40-ft. boat. My address will be Capt. Hardy's Sea Inn, No. 12 Cedar St.

Last mo. at the Claridge Apt., I met your old friend Loris. She's an atty. now for Greshem and Co., and likes her work. She came to my show at the Terrace Theater on Green Ct. and enjoyed it, even though it lasted about an hr. longer than it should have. My magic rope got tangled up in Mrs. Quinto's hair, and then my rabbit fell into a gal. of buttermilk, so it took about 45 min. to get all that straightened out! But the audience loved it, and I'm doing another show there a wk. from next Sat.

Hope all at our house on Grover Blvd. is fine, and that you and Mom are doing all right without me this yr. I'll be home in Dec. Until then, write me in care of the Dept. of Magicians, Ottawa, Can.

Love from your devoted brother,
Humberto

a.m. _____     atty. _____
Sat. _____     Capt. _____
Ct. _____      Dept. _____
ft. _____      min. _____
hr. _____      Mrs. _____
n. _____       Blvd. _____
St. _____      Mr. _____
Apt. _____     no. _____
Can. _____     Co. _____
Dec. _____     Dr. _____
gal. _____     Is. _____
mo. _____      yr. _____
Aug. _____     St. _____
wk. _____

# WHAT'S THE WEATHER?

Find and circle 30 compound words in the cloud. Words have been hidden horizontally, vertically, and diagonally, but never backwards.

```
W I N D B L O W N W H E T H E R S
I T S H E S T O R M B O U N D W U
N E K A T N H E R R I F S N A C N
D O Y L D O O W A R W R U H Y E L
S T L H E W R A I N C O A T L S I
T R I T H F E W N N B S E H I N G
O A G T H A E R B W D T I U G O H
R S H A I L S T O R M B H N H W T
M R T F O L T N W W E I R D T F H
C A W O O L S L W E A T T E H L O
L I H G H G E R T H E E N R A A A
O N I B W E H A T M H A U S I K R
U F R O S T W O R K P O E T L E F
D A L U R W H O R W P A T O S E R
B L W N V E T R O N T H E R T W O
U L I D E S A D W T H E R M O W S
R H N E N S N O W S T O R M N T T
S H D I E I D S U N S H I N E R W
T E A L W E A T H E R M A N I K E
I R A I N D R O P T O R N O T ■
```

The leftover letters from the puzzle spell a weather message. Figure it out and write it here.

_____

_____

# IT'S NOT A PRETTY PICTURE!

Write the story this picture tells. Use the back of this sheet if you need more room.

_____

_____

_____

_____

_____

_____

_____

_____

_____

_____

_____

# THRIFTY
# TIMOTHY
# THORNGILL

Read the paragraph below all the way through. Then write one of the words from the balloons in each blank to complete the sentences correctly.

Timothy Thorngill is a _____ teenager. He works hard to _____ of ways to save his money. But sometimes he does surprising _____ . Last Tuesday his uncle Thomas gave him _____ dollars to buy a fancy cake and ice cream to celebrate his _____ birthday. Timothy _____ of his brother and sister, and decided to use the money to make them happy. Instead of buying the fancy treats, he used the money to purchase _____ tickets for his whole family. Then he made popcorn and a _____ of lemonade, and invited all the kids on the block to his party.

think
thought

things
thirty

thermos
thrifty

theater
thirteenth

# SCRAMBLED EGGS

Find and circle the names of 36 animals that lay eggs. The names go up and down, across, or on a slant, but never backwards or upside down.

The leftover letters spell the name of an egg-laying animal that roamed the earth long ago, but is now extinct.

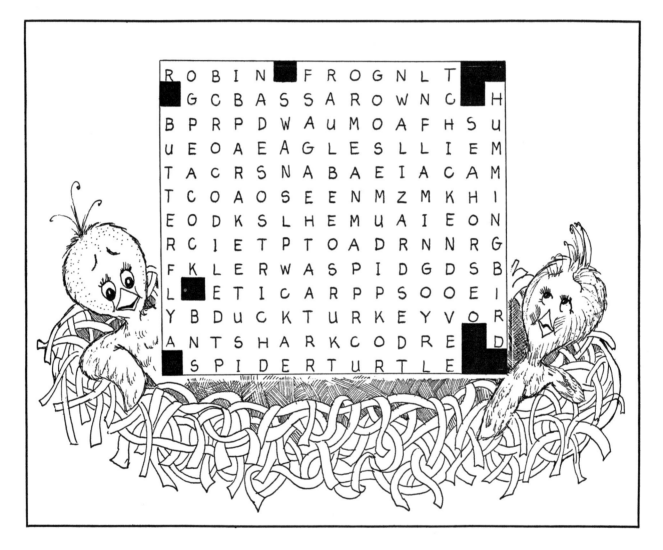

```
R  O  B  I  N     F  R  O  G  N  L  T
   G  C  B  A  S  S  A  R  O  W  N  C     H
B  P  R  P  D  W  A  U  M  O  A  F  H  S  U
U  E  O  A  E  A  G  L  E  S  L  L  I  E  M
T  A  C  R  S  N  A  B  A  E  I  A  C  A  M
T  C  O  A  O  S  E  E  N  M  Z  M  K  H  I
E  O  D  K  S  L  H  E  M  U  A  I  E  O  N
R  C  I  E  T  P  T  O  A  D  R  N  N  R  G
F  K  L  E  R  W  A  S  P  I  D  G  D  S  B
L     E  T  I  C  A  R  P  P  P  S  O  O  E  I
Y  B  D  U  C  K  T  U  R  K  E  Y  V  O  R
A  N  T  S  H  A  R  K  C  O  D  R  E     D
   S  P  I  D  E  R  T  U  R  T  L  E
```

Write the name of the animal that the leftover letters spell.

_____

How many scrambled-egg breakfasts do you think just 1 of that animal's eggs would make? _____

# TALE OF A TACKY TROLL

It's clean-up day for Trixie the tacky troll. Her mother has said that she definitely will not be allowed to go to the troll picnic until her room is in order. The problem is that she did not put things away in their proper places because she was lazy.

Draw an arrow from the out-of-place item on each shelf to the shelf on which it belongs.

Draw in 1 more item on each shelf that does belong.

# DIFFERENT WORDS, DIFFERENT STORY

Rewrite the story using the correct antonym from the box for each underlined word. Give the story a surprise ending.

Words to use:

| | | | |
|---|---|---|---|
| happy | young | quickly | light |
| quiet | harmless | small | from |
| soothing | strong | downward | |

As the <u>sad</u> <u>old</u> gnome <u>slowly</u> entered the forest, the moon cast a <u>dark</u> and <u>frightening</u> glow. Suddenly he heard a <u>loud</u> sound. Just then, he spotted a <u>dangerous</u>-looking vulture perched in a <u>huge</u> tree. As the gnome moved <u>to</u> the tree, the vulture spread its <u>weak</u> wings and soared straight <u>upward</u>.

# MARK THE HOMONYM TRAIL

For years, the wicked wizard has been trying to steal Marilee Monster's jewels. After many close calls, Marilee decided to bury her jewels in the Homonym Desert. Since the wizard doesn't understand homonyms, Marilee decided that would be the safest place.

Marilee drew a map so her sister could find the jewels if she needed them, but her sister doesn't understand homonyms either. Now she needs the jewels. Help Marilee's sister follow the maze (map) and find the jewels by writing in the correct homonym for each word written below the sentence on each sign.

# TEST YOUR WORD KNOWLEDGE

Read this paragraph carefully. Then complete the word knowledge test.

1. The arid desert baked relentlessly under the fierce noonday sun.
2. Tumbleweeds and desert grasses looked forever dead.   3. Even the cacti appeared shriveled and dry.   4. The whole area gave off a dismal feeling.   5. The weary traveler could see no signs of life anywhere.
6. He wondered where all the desert animals were hiding.   7. He wondered too how much longer he could go on without water or shade.   8. Suddenly this desert expedition seemed to be a very poor idea indeed.

1.  Circle the phrase that means almost the same thing as **relentlessly** in sentence 1.

without ceasing              forever after              some of the time

2.  Circle the word that could best be substituted for **dead** in sentence 2.

withered                      shivered                      frosted

3.  Circle the word that means the opposite of **shriveled** as it is used in sentence 3.

exploded                      expanded                      expressed

4.  Circle the word that best could be substituted for **dismal** in sentence 4.

distant                       depressing                    desperate

5.  Circle the word that best tells how the traveler felt.

angry                         tired                         unhappy

6.  Circle the phrase that means the opposite of **wondered** as it is used in sentence 7.

knew for sure                 began to question            thought about

7.  Circle the word that best could be substituted for **expedition** in sentence 8.

invitation                    recovery                      journey

# THE INCREDIBLE
# MATH MACHINE

In your math textbook, locate 20 math terms that are used often. Look up the meaning of any word you do not know. Then write your words in the Incredible Math Machine.

Filling the machine with key math words will help you "blast off" to better understanding of math!

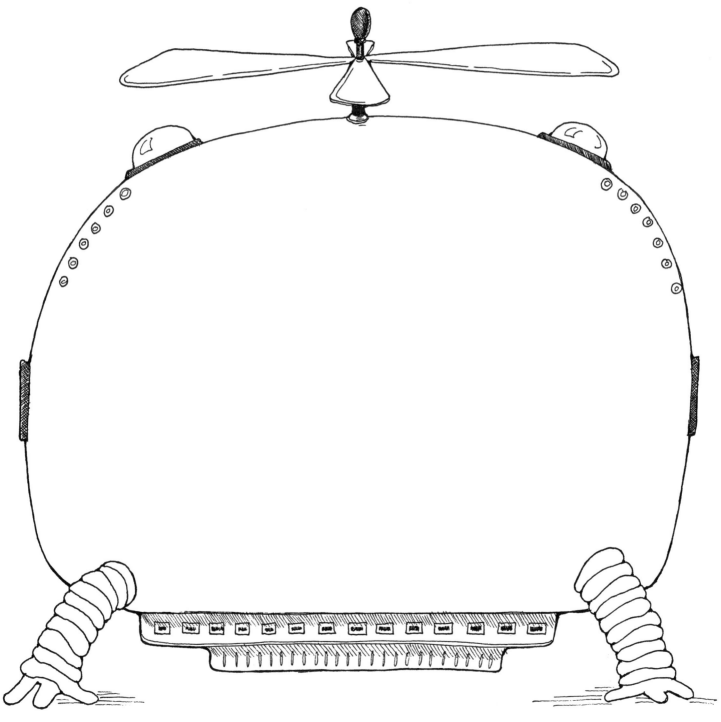

# PIXIE POWER

Fill each blank below with the best descriptive word from the list. Use each word only once.

Words to use:
marvelous    cunning      horrifying       evil
lonely       flaming      unsuspecting     pudgy
desolate     confused     bewildered       eerie
ruthless     fastidious   superstitious    mischievous
                                           unfortunate

1. Pixies are believed to be tiny, _____ fairies who have _____ red hair, pointed ears, _____ faces, and turned-up noses.

2. Legend has it that pixies love to mislead _____ travelers by causing them to become _____ and _____ .

3. _____ travelers tricked by pixies can escape by turning their clothes inside out, as pixies are very _____ about dress.

4. Being trapped by pixies would be a _____ experience for a _____ traveler on a dark and _____ road.

5. Pixies are also accused of being _____ and _____ horse thieves.

6. Some _____ people nail iron horseshoes above their barn doors to keep the _____ pixies away.

7. Even so, wouldn't it be a _____ experience to meet a pixie in all its _____ splendor?

# A SCARY STORY

Read about Helga and Nars. Select the words from the word bank to complete each sentence. Write 2 sentences to give the story a surprise ending.

Helga and Nars never should have left for home so late on a day like this. The blizzard was becoming more _____ by the minute. Because their crippled mother was at home alone, they really _____ for her safety. As the blinding wind and driving snow became stronger, Nars became _____ . He crammed his icy hands into his pockets, however, and pushed _____ ahead. He was trying _____ to keep Helga from _____ . As Helga followed in his footsteps, her heart pounded _____ . All she could think of was how _____ and cold she felt. Because the snow had completely wiped away the path, both children felt _____ and _____ . As darkness approached, even brave Nars was beginning to feel _____ .

_____

_____

_____

_____

_____

Words to use:
bewildered
bravely
confused
desperate

desperately
feared
frantically

frightening
panicking
terrified
wretched

# ON STAGE

Study the stage scene below.

Select from each word list 3 words that you think will best create an interesting character.

Draw faces to reflect the personalities you have created.

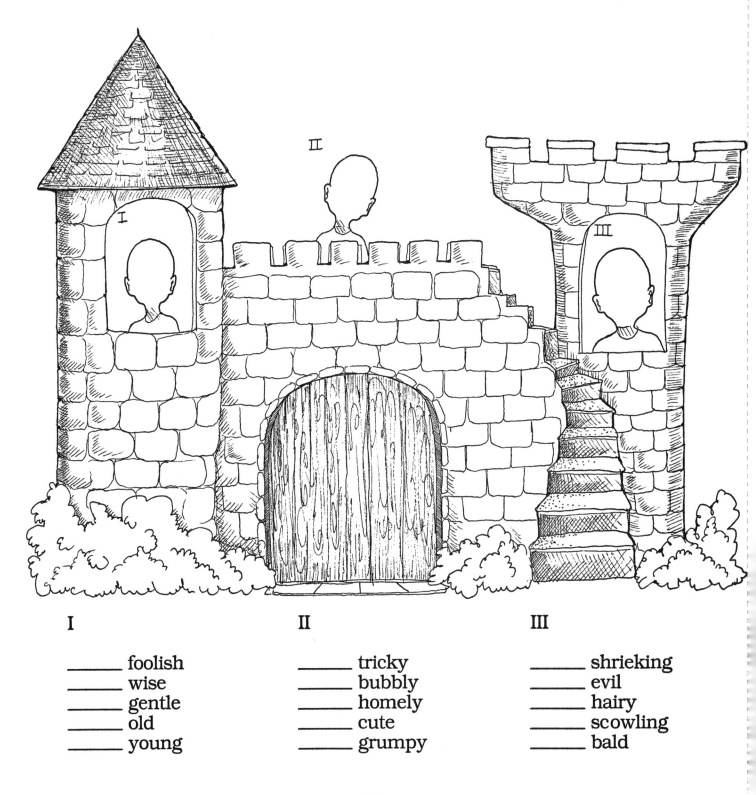

**I**

_____ foolish
_____ wise
_____ gentle
_____ old
_____ young

**II**

_____ tricky
_____ bubbly
_____ homely
_____ cute
_____ grumpy

**III**

_____ shrieking
_____ evil
_____ hairy
_____ scowling
_____ bald

# SAY WHAT YOU MEAN!

In the fewest words possible, write what you think each of these sayings means.

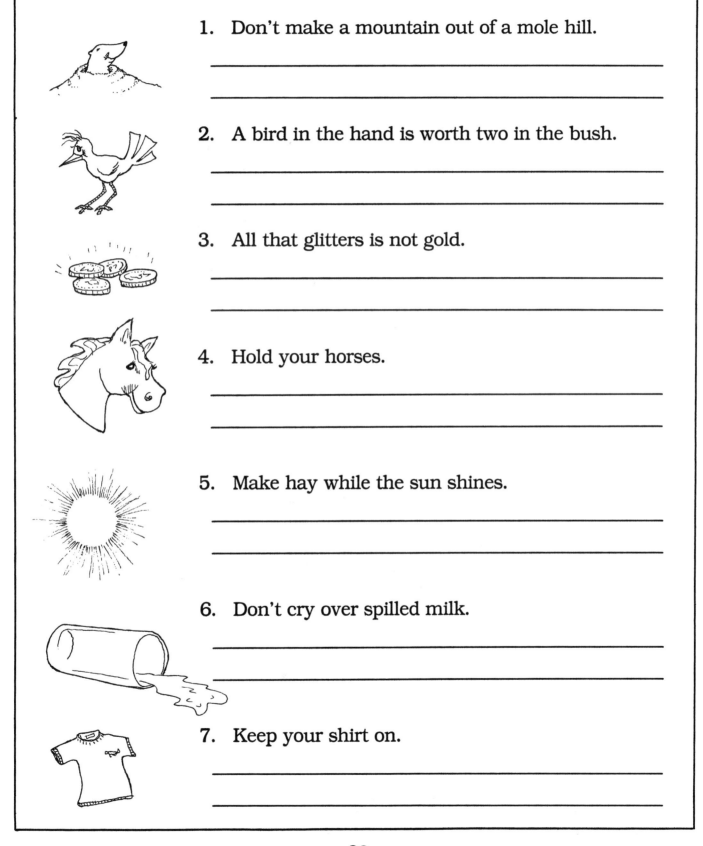

1.  Don't make a mountain out of a mole hill.

   _____

   _____

2.  A bird in the hand is worth two in the bush.

   _____

   _____

3.  All that glitters is not gold.

   _____

   _____

4.  Hold your horses.

   _____

   _____

5.  Make hay while the sun shines.

   _____

   _____

6.  Don't cry over spilled milk.

   _____

   _____

7.  Keep your shirt on.

   _____

   _____

# SENTENCE SPECIAL

Combine 1 word or phrase from each of the 3 columns to make sentences.

Words or phrases may be used more than once as long as they are not used twice in the same sentence.

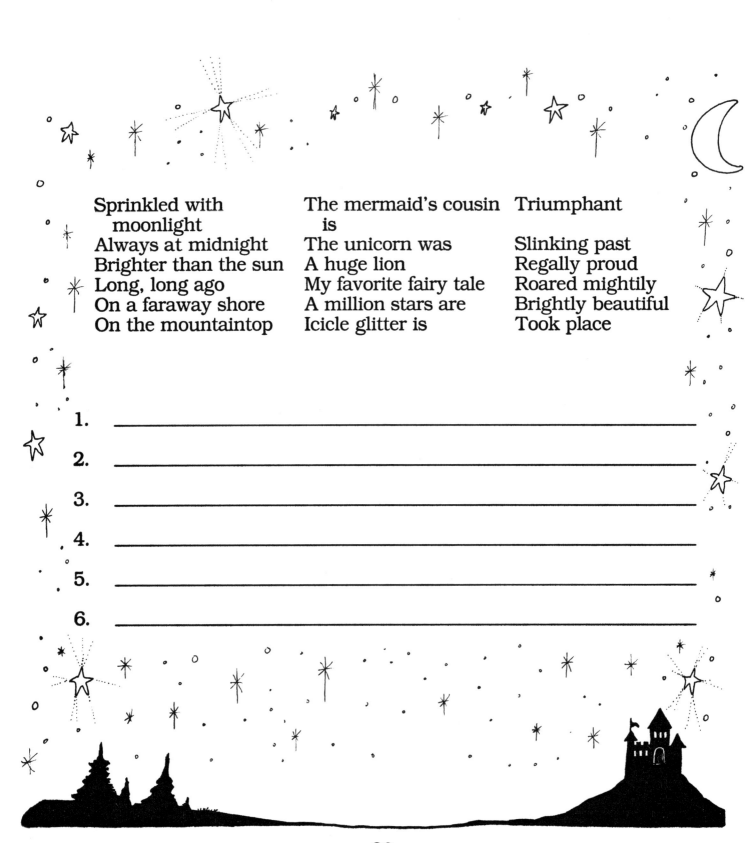

| | | |
|---|---|---|
| Sprinkled with moonlight | The mermaid's cousin is | Triumphant |
| Always at midnight | The unicorn was | Slinking past |
| Brighter than the sun | A huge lion | Regally proud |
| Long, long ago | My favorite fairy tale | Roared mightily |
| On a faraway shore | A million stars are | Brightly beautiful |
| On the mountaintop | Icicle glitter is | Took place |

1. _____

2. _____

3. _____

4. _____

5. _____

6. _____

# IN THE MOOD

Here are some story excerpts in which the author tried to create a definite feeling or mood. Read each one carefully. Identify the feeling or mood by drawing a line from the excerpt to the picture that shows the same mood. Then reread each story and underline the key words (the ones that let you know the mood of the excerpt).

1) The beautiful princess began to look pale and miserable as each day she pressed her tear-stained face against the bars covering the tiny window of the dungeon where she was being held captive.

2) As the sun broke through the clouds and shed its brilliance over the tall trees and beautifully blooming vines, the whole forest took on a look of golden radiance.

3) The shoemaker could hardly believe his eyes when he awoke to find his whole shop filled with neat rows of carefully crafted shoes. The little space was spic and span, giving it an air of order and cheerfulness.

4) Prudence Porcupine did her very best to appear comfortable at the elegant table spread with glowing candles, sparkling crystal, and glittering silver. "If I can only eat without choking!" she prayed silently.

# A WORD ON MOODS

Underline the word on the line beneath each sentence that best describes the mood of that sentence.

1.  Queen Sylvia beamed with delight as she looked around her newly decorated throne room.

    contented                happy                uneasy

2.  The horses were neighing and stamping as they moved jerkily from side to side in the humid, sultry stable.

    orderly                tranquil                restless

3.  Hans gritted his teeth, clutched the stick he carried and forced himself to move cautiously forward as he heard the hissing and growling grow louder.

    fearful                peaceful                angry

4.  Tinker Toad jumped high in the air, did a few cartwheels and continued to flip flop about the grassy pasture.

    lazy                playful                sinister

Read the sentences again. Illustrate the one of your choice.

# AN EVIL OGRE

The Ogre of the Dead Forest stole the words that complete these sentences and locked them in his dungeon. Set them free by figuring out which ones go where and writing them in the correct blanks.

1.  **Web** is to _____ as **lair** is to **dragon.**

2.  **Mischief** is to an **elf** as _____ is to a **troll.**

3.  **Nymph** is to **beautiful** as **goblin** is to _____ .

4.  **Toad's tongue** is to a witch's **potion** as **oil of light** is to a fairy's
    _____ .

5.  **Making toys** is to **dwarves** as **making trouble** is to _____ .

6.  A **poisoned apple** is to an _____ as a **prince's kiss** is to a **good spell.**

7.  A **pot of gold** is to a _____ as a **horde of gold** is to a **dragon.**

8.  _____ is to **fairies** as **black smoke** is to **warlocks.**

9.  **Fire** is to a **dragon** as a _____ is to a **knight.**

10. **Dungeon** is to a _____ as a **castle** is to a **king.**

stardust   spider
           sword
prisoner
           goblins
evil spell
leprechaun   ugly
nectar   danger

# WERNER AND VICTOR

An *oxymoron* is a combination of words that seem to contradict each other, such as **laughing unhappily.**

Find and underline the 9 oxymorons in this story.

One day, Werner the wise fool and Victor the valiant coward decided to visit the city of Niccoo. As they followed their road through a dark forest, Victor asked Werner to take the lead so he could guard the rear. Werner thought Victor should go first, as his bright sword would frighten away any beasts or thieves in the woods. But with a sad smile, Victor said, "Yes, but present fears are less than horrible imaginings!" Werner saw much wisdom in this, so he went first.

They walked on quickly through the forest. Suddenly Werner halted. They had come to the river, and the bridge was out! Ever the happy pessimist, Victor sat down and began to wail, "We'll never cross this river! We're stuck here forever! This is the beginning of the end!"

"No, no," said Werner. "Here is the solution, hiding in plain sight. We'll just push this tree over, and it will make a bridge across the river for us." And he began to push with all his strength.

Victor jumped up and pushed him aside. "I'll chop the tree down with my sword!" he said, and began to chop with his bright blade.

Just then, a tiny giant appeared in a poof of black smoke. In a voice like quiet thunder he rumbled, "Who are you and why do you chop on my tree?"

Victor's shaking knees gave way, and he fell to the ground. Werner quickly explained their problem, and begged the giant for help. But the two trembling travelers looked so funny that the giant laughed and laughed until happy tears filled his eyes. By mistake, he bumped into the very tree that Victor had been chopping on, and it fell right over the river! Werner grabbed Victor and dragged him over the tree bridge, and they both ran until the laughing giant was far behind and they were out of the forest. Soon they could see the city of Niccoo just down the road. They were safe at last!

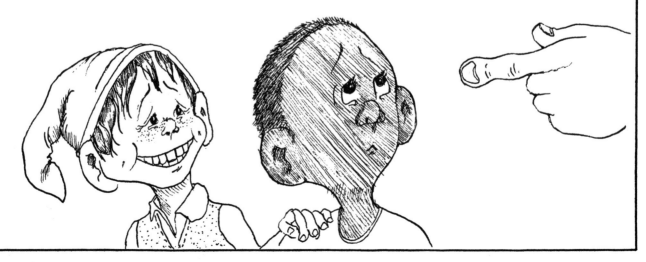

# SEVEN CHILDREN TO DESCRIBE

Select a word from the list below to "fit" each child described in the poem. Then use your dictionary or thesaurus to find one more word that could be used to describe each child.

Monday's child is fair of face;
Tuesday's child is full of grace;
Wednesday's child is full of woe;
Thursday's child has far to go;
Friday's child works hard for a living;
Saturday's child is loving and giving;
And the child that is born on the Sabbath day
Is bonnie and blythe and good and gay.

WORD LIST:
industrious     cheerful     pretty     sad
        graceful     adventuresome     generous

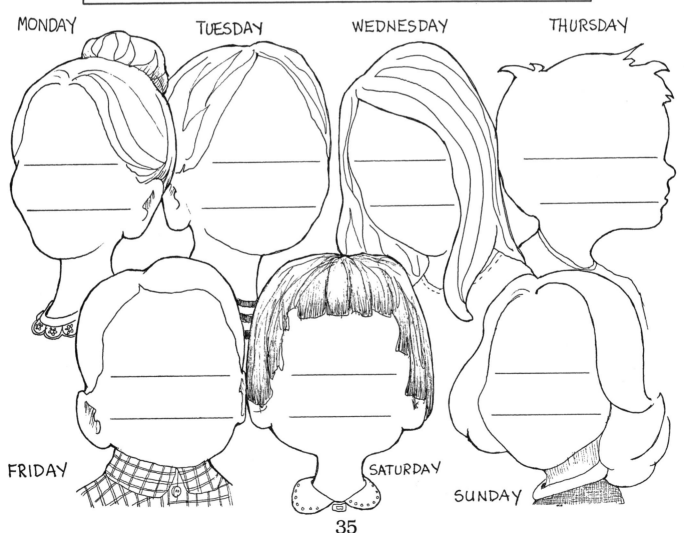

MONDAY     TUESDAY     WEDNESDAY     THURSDAY

FRIDAY     SATURDAY     SUNDAY

# MIDNIGHT MADNESS

Make this story more exciting by substituting a word from the list below for each underlined word. Use each word only once.

It was a dark, stormy night in Metropolis. The city lights shone

_____  _____  _____  _____

wickedly in the wet streets, and the only night sounds to be heard

_____  _____  _____

were the crying of police cars and the howling of ambulances.

_____  _____

A rickety bus plodded around a corner and stopped in front of a

_____  _____

dilapidated building. The neon sign above the door was blinking on and

_____  _____

off in the night "Th  City H tel." Full trash cans lined the hotel

_____  _____  _____  _____

sidewalk; their tops fell to the ground with harsh noises as wandering

_____  _____  _____  _____  _____

cats and dogs sneaked through the trash.

_____  _____

As she sat on the bus, Joyce stared tiredly out the window at the

_____

sad scene with a falling heart. "I don't want to stay here," she

_____  _____

thought. "This hotel is old and shabby, and I'll bet it's dirty inside. It

_____  _____

doesn't matter that our whole bunch will be collected. This area looks

_____  _____  _____

unsafe to me. I question whether our guide has stayed here previously.

_____  _____  _____

Surely not! This place is just awful!"

_____

Words to use:
darkness; screaming; wonder; edged; dreary; group; sinking; crashes; glittered; vile; wearily; concrete; tempestuous; together; lids; filthy; before; evilly; stray; neighborhood; rain-washed; run-down; rubbish; seedy; dangerous; depressing; raucous; overflowing; lumbered; wailing; noises; creaking; skulked; flashing.

# WORD-ABILITY WIZARD

Finding words in a bigger word is a game that helps people test their word ability. Without using contractions, proper nouns or slang, make as many words as you can from this word:

I N V E S T I G A T I O N

To rate as a real word-ability wizard, find at least 40 words. Try to find 4-letter words, 5-letter words, 6-letter words and even some 7- and 8-letter words!

If you had fun with this one, try P R E S T I D I G I T A T I O N !!!

37

# WITH WORDS IN MIND

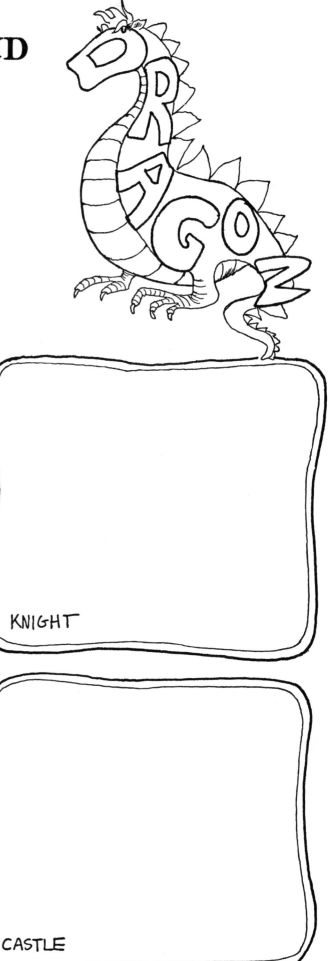

Certain words instantly bring pictures into your mind, just as certain pictures make you think of words that go with them. Can you combine words and pictures into a new art form?

Here is the way one person sees the word "dragon." Now read these words, and draw your own pictures in the spaces below.

SWORD

KNIGHT

PRINCESS

CASTLE

# WORDS ON THE LINE

Ask a friend to play this game with you.
The game rules are:

1. Write 5 words on each line below.
2. Each word must begin with the last letter of the word just before it.
3. Try to use words containing the most letters possible.
4. Each player gets 1 point for each letter correctly used.
5. The player with the most points wins the game.

EXAMPLE:  mercury _yesterday - yourself - found - dollar - random_

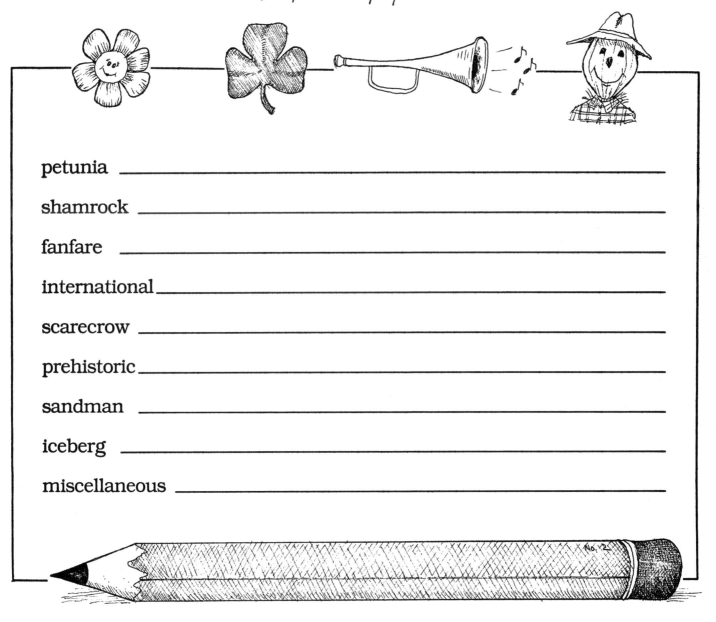

petunia _____

shamrock _____

fanfare _____

international _____

scarecrow _____

prehistoric _____

sandman _____

iceberg _____

miscellaneous _____

P.S.   If you want to play this game by yourself, set a goal of the number of points you want to reach, and see how close you come to your goal.

# INDEPENDENT READING

## SKILLS

So ride away the Unicorn
To know the world that was,
The world the way it is today,
Or what is yet to come.

# UP THE BEANSTALK

Climb the ladder with Jack!
Read Jack's story. Then fill in the **who, what, when, where, why,** and **how** ladder.

Although Jack meant to sell his mother's cow, he traded it for some bean seeds instead. When his mother threw the seeds out, they took root and grew into a tremendous beanstalk. Jack climbed it, and found a giant's castle at the top. When he got inside the castle, the wicked giant tried to kill and eat Jack, but Jack managed to escape down the beanstalk with the giant's treasures. The giant followed him, but Jack reached the bottom first, grabbed an axe, and chopped down the beanstalk. The giant crashed down into the earth with the beanstalk and vanished forever. Jack and his mother kept the treasures and lived happily ever after.

WHO

WHAT

WHEN

WHERE

WHY

HOW

# THE KNIGHT'S JOURNEY

Read the story. Underline the topic sentence in each paragraph.

The Silver Knight sat astride his faithful steed, his polished armor glinting in the sun. He had left the castle before daybreak on a mission for His Royal Majesty, King Peter the Peaceful. The message he carried was to be delivered to the King of Tarrn, for it was an invitation for the king and all his lords and ladies to attend a feast in celebration of ten years of peace between the two lands. By noon the Silver Knight had crossed the border into Tarrn, and was trying to decide which of the unmarked roads would lead him to his destination — the Great Hall of Tarrn.

Suddenly he heard someone approaching on horseback. He closed his visor, raised his shield, and made ready to draw his sword. Although there was peace between the two countries, the Silver Knight knew there were many other dangers, such as thieves and cruel highwaymen, that made it necessary to use great care when traveling alone. Quietly guiding his horse off the pathway to the cover of a great old oak tree, the knight waited anxiously to discover the identity of the approaching rider.

Into the clearing before him emerged a splendid white horse, fitted with a halter of ostrich plumes and sparkling jewels. On the horse there sat a knight of the Great Hall of Tarrn. The Silver Knight could tell from the horse's fittings and the knight's shield that this was the king's own messenger. What could his mission be? The Silver Knight realized that this rider must be intending to deliver a message to his own King Peter! With this thought, he urged his horse forward into the clearing and approached the Knight of Tarrn with a smile and a palm upraised in a token of peace.

44

# GOBLINS FOR CHRISTMAS

Read about the Christmas goblins. Complete the sentences without reading the story again. Then reread the story to check your answers.

Long ago, many people in Iceland told stories of the Christmas goblins. Children were told that the goblins appeared one at a time for 13 days before Christmas. The goblins were said to leave one at a time on each of the 13 days after Christmas. They were described as big and clumsy. People rushed around hiding Christmas goodies and making sure the house was goblin-safe. All sorts of spills, rips, and stains were blamed on these poor, ugly creatures. Storytellers say that many tales were told of the Christmas goblins, but not one person ever told of actually seeing one.

Circle the letter of the best answer.
1. The main idea of this story is
   (a) Christmas goblins
   (b) Christmas in Iceland
   (c) How Icelandic children celebrate Christmas
2. The goblins were believed to stay in the house for
   (a) 13 days
   (b) 25 days
   (c) 27 days
3. Stories of the Christmas goblins were
   (a) true
   (b) half true
   (c) tall tales

# NUMBER, PLEASE

Use the telephone directory to find a name and a telephone number to complete each sentence.

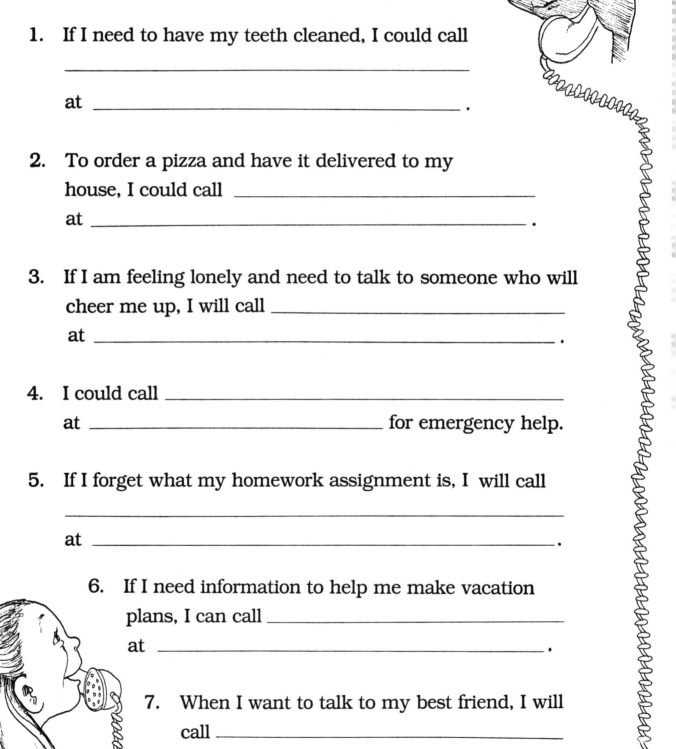

1. If I need to have my teeth cleaned, I could call

   _____

   at _____ .

2. To order a pizza and have it delivered to my house, I could call _____

   at _____ .

3. If I am feeling lonely and need to talk to someone who will cheer me up, I will call _____

   at _____ .

4. I could call _____

   at _____ for emergency help.

5. If I forget what my homework assignment is, I will call

   _____

   at _____ .

6. If I need information to help me make vacation plans, I can call _____

   at _____ .

7. When I want to talk to my best friend, I will call _____

   at _____ .

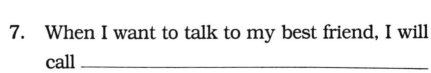

46

# THE ELIXIR OF INVISIBILITY

Read the sentences below, paying careful attention to the details. Circle and label the portion in each sentence that tells **who, what, when, where, why,** and **how.**

1. Late one night in his dusty study, an old man carefully poured strange ingredients into a small flask to make a magic potion.

2. For many years, he had labored all alone in that room, trying to make an Elixir of Invisibility.

3. With such an elixir, the old man could go where and when he pleased, for no one would be able to see him or know that he was there.

4. He especially wanted to be able to hide from his wife when she nagged him crossly to do some handy work around the house.

5. After stirring the mixture for some time, he lifted the flask with trembling hands and put it to his lips to taste it.

Extra: What do you think happened? Finish this story on the back of this page.

# DETAIL SELECTION

A few very important details have been left out of this story.
Write a word or phrase from the Detail Selection List in each blank.
Write **who, what, where, when,** or **why** next to each word or
phrase from the list as it is used.
Then write 3 sentences to give the story a surprise ending.

Detail Selection List

strange adventure _____          large imagination _____
Timmy Thacker _____              hot day _____
muddy river bank _____           standing _____

_____ _____ was a very small

boy with a very large imagination. If he had stayed home as his mother

told him to, he never would have been _____ on that

_____ _____ _____ on that

_____ _____ . It was because of his

_____ _____ that the _____

_____ took place. _____

_____

_____

_____

_____

_____

_____

_____

_____

# BALLOW'S DILEMMA

Read the sentences below. Number them 1-9 to show the order in which they should appear.

_____ Angus told him that a coyote had been seen in the new pasture.

_____ Today the sheep would go to a new pasture.

_____ He was up and dressed before sunrise.

_____ Should he take a chance on moving the sheep today, or should he wait for the hunters to capture the coyote?

_____ This was the day that Ballow the shepherd had been waiting for.

_____ Angus also said that a party of hunters was searching for the coyote.

_____ With his lunch bag and stick, he headed for the pasture.

_____ With his heart beating furiously, Ballow tried to decide what to do.

_____ Along the way, he met his friend Angus.

Recopy the story in the proper sequence.

_____

_____

_____

_____

_____

_____

_____

_____

_____

_____

_____

# HOW DOES IT END?

Read the sentences below. Number them to show the order in which they should appear in the story.

Write 3 more sentences of your own to give the story a surprise ending.

_____ She had a lovely voice and took great pleasure in singing beautiful ballads as she worked.

_____ The daughter loved her father very much, but she longed for the friendship of people her own age.

_____ The old man was very sweet, but he was blind in one eye and completely deaf.

_____ Since her mother's death, the daughter had not been able to leave her father alone in the poor home in which they lived.

_____ Long ago in a land beyond the Sea of Sassafras, there lived a kind old man and his beautiful daughter.

_____ They lived mostly on fruits and berries from the forest, vegetables from their meager garden, and a few eggs from their hens.

_____ One day as she was singing in the garden, a handsome young man on a beautiful white horse rode up and asked for a drink of water.

_____ They had not been into the village or talked with anyone but each other for many years.

_____

_____

_____

_____

_____

_____

_____

_____

_____

_____

# FABLE FRAMES

Below are 9 frames from 2 different fables. Cut out all the frames and decide which story each is from. Then put the 2 sets in order. Number them (1A-5A and 1B-4B) to show the order you have put them in.

Keep a record of your reading by writing titles of books as you read them.

Challenge a friend to a book race by trying to see whose bookshelf is filled first.

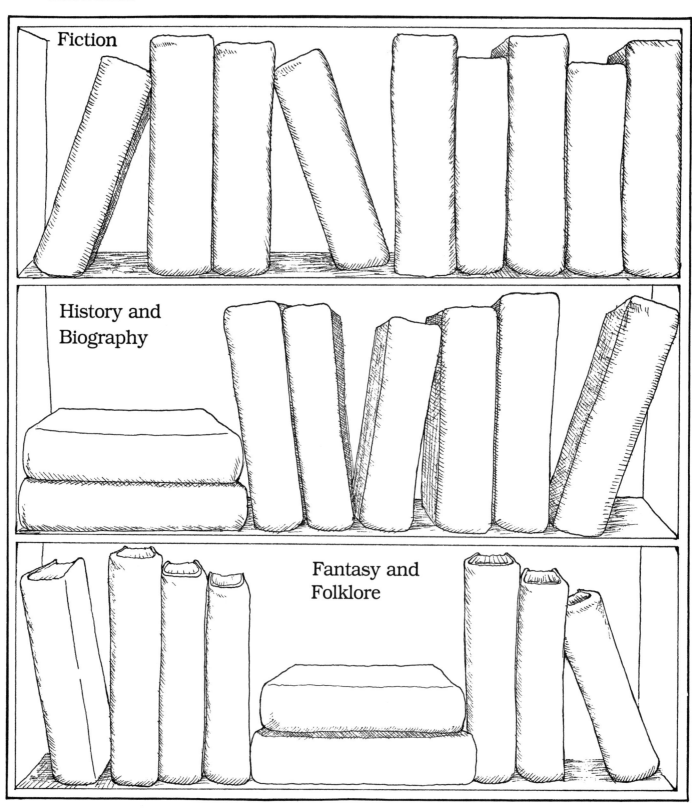

Fiction

History and Biography

Fantasy and Folklore

# STORM WARNING

Zerda and Gaslop were cruising along through space on their flight home. All was quiet on the Turasian spaceship, and Zerda was taking a nap as she sat beside the telecommunicator. Suddenly the machine flashed on, and the following information appeared on the screen.

You are approaching Sector VX6, Square #7 at 80,000 megaquarps per second, which will put you at the Sector border in 23.6 minutes. Although previously a neutral sector with light traffic and no weather, Sector VX6, Square #7 is now the center of a nuclear-ion tornado. Winds have been measured by monitoring equipment at 14,728.63 velosparks per second, which your ship is not equipped to handle. The force of the negative and positive nuclear ions has created a magnetic whirlwind, which is presently sucking in all spaceships in the surrounding vectors. We recommend that you summarize this information and feed it into your Skyway Path computer to set a new course away from the storm.

Summarize the information here so Zerda can plug it into the computer and get away from the storm.

_____

_____

_____

_____

_____

_____

# LET THE GNOMES KNOW

Read all about the big celebration being planned for the gnomes. Then help the gnomes by writing a short ad for the Gnomeville *News*. You may use only 3 sentences, so make sure to include only the most important information.

Six weeks ago, the Chief Gnome appointed eight gnome lieutenants to the planning committee for the Winter Moon Festival. Every Thursday night since then, the committee has met to work out the details of the celebration. They have decided to start the party at 10:00 p.m. next Friday night, the 13th of Gnovember, at Numb Skull Hill. All the gnomes in the gnomedom are invited, and should wear costumes and bring musical instruments. First, second, and third prizes will be given for the ugliest costumes worn and the weirdest music made with an instrument. Prizes will be awarded at midnight by the Chief Gnome, and the king and queen of the festival will be introduced at that time also. Folk dancing, feasting and frolicking will follow these festivities until daybreak, when all good gnomes must be back underground.

# WHAT NEXT?

Finish the following picture sequences by "reading" them and drawing in your own conclusions.

# HOW FAMOUS IS FAMOUS?

In the Question Box, write the name of a famous woman that you admire who is no longer living (athlete, author, world leader, humanitarian, other).

Locate factual information about this woman in the encyclopedia.

How many paragraphs of information did you find about this woman?
_____

Do you think the number of paragraphs indicates how important or famous this woman was? _____

If you had been in charge of the encyclopedia, would you have included more, less, or just about the same amount of information about this woman? _____

In what year was the woman born? _____

In what year did the woman die? _____

Why was the woman famous? _____

_____

Do you think the woman would become famous for doing the very same thing if she were living now rather than then? _____

# TELL IT YOUR WAY

Write an ending for this story.

Once upon a time, a poor princess was lost in a forest. At nightfall a big storm blew up, and the princess tried to find some shelter. As she stumbled along in the rain, she suddenly saw a tremendous castle ahead. She ran up to it and knocked loudly at the gate until the guards let her in.

The guards took her to the king and queen. She told them that she was lost, and asked for help. The royal couple welcomed her and told her she could stay at their palace. She thanked them, and went with the queen's lady-in-waiting to get some dry clothes.

At dinner that night, the princess met the king and queen's son who was home visiting his parents. They fell madly in love, and immediately made plans to marry.

The only problem that they had to overcome was _____

_____

_____

_____

_____

_____

_____

_____

_____

_____

_____

_____

_____

_____

57

# HOW BIG IS THIS BIG DEAL?

Read the ad that Bixie Big-Deal placed in the classified section of the Fairy Forest Newspaper. Underline the sentences that you think are facts. Circle the sentences that you think are opinions.

The brand-new, Super-Duper Fairy Wand is now available at Treasure Troves, Inc., throughout the whole fairy kingdom. You must buy this fantastic, world famous, one-of-a-kind magic wand. This newly invented wand is rainbow-colored, and folds to fit into a standard-size fairy knapsack. This wand is made of durable materials and is finely crafted. It comes with a lifetime guarantee. No self-respecting ambitious young fairy can afford to go into the world without this wand.

It is believed that the Super-Duper Fairy Wand will ward off evil spirits, guard against unpleasant odors and ensure the owner prosperity and good health.

RUSH to your nearest Treasure Trove Shop to buy your Super-Duper Fairy Wand today! Quantities are limited — tomorrow may be too late!!

# CARELESS CLARA CLARK

The pictures in Column I show something that happened to Careless Clara Clark. Each picture in Column II shows an effect of one of the happenings.

Draw a line to connect each "cause" picture with the correct "effect" picture.

I

II

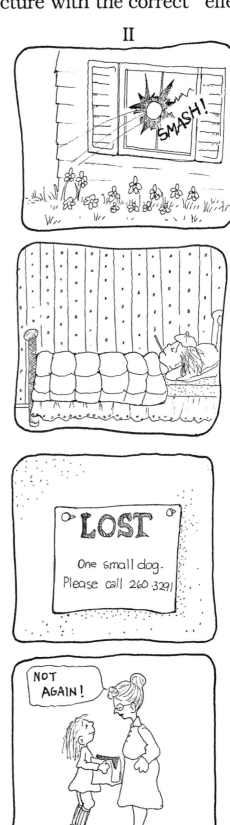

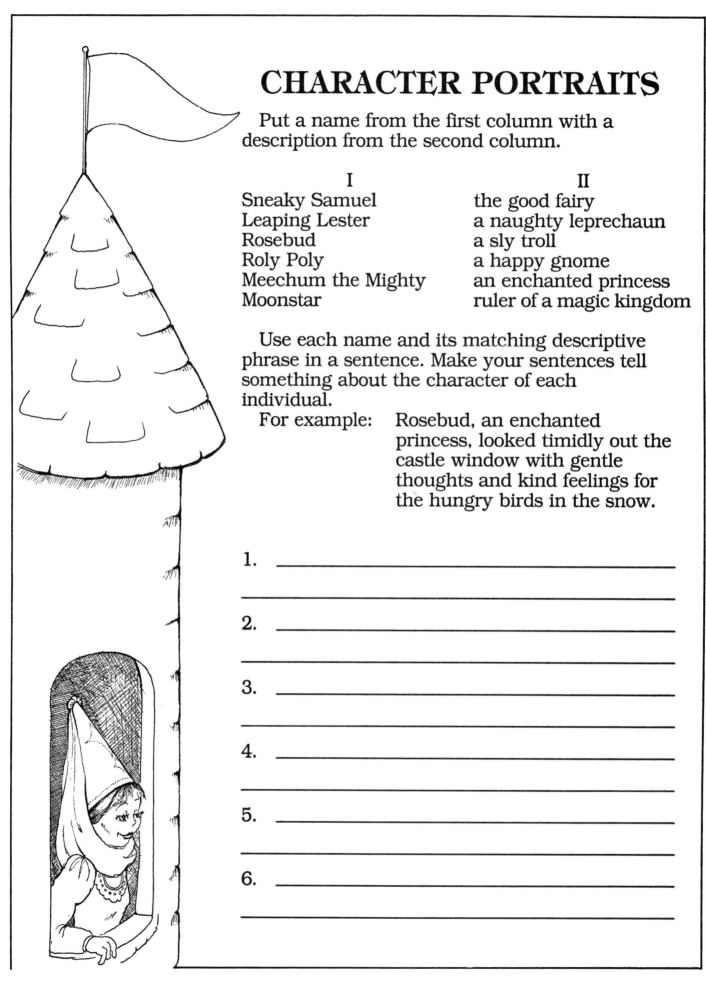

# CHARACTER PORTRAITS

Put a name from the first column with a description from the second column.

| I | II |
|---|---|
| Sneaky Samuel | the good fairy |
| Leaping Lester | a naughty leprechaun |
| Rosebud | a sly troll |
| Roly Poly | a happy gnome |
| Meechum the Mighty | an enchanted princess |
| Moonstar | ruler of a magic kingdom |

Use each name and its matching descriptive phrase in a sentence. Make your sentences tell something about the character of each individual.

For example:   Rosebud, an enchanted princess, looked timidly out the castle window with gentle thoughts and kind feelings for the hungry birds in the snow.

1. _____

_____

2. _____

_____

3. _____

_____

4. _____

_____

5. _____

_____

6. _____

_____

# AS YOU SEE IT

Certain phrases automatically bring visual images to mind. These images are usually triggered by personal experiences, and may be very different for any two people.

Read each phrase below, and quickly draw the very first picture that comes to mind. Ask a friend to do the same thing, and compare your finished drawings.

| | |
|---|---|
| *King of the Road* | "in the groove" |
| **Sugar 'n Spice & Everything Nice** | PACK UP YOUR TROUBLEs |

# ORGANIZING A NEWSSTAND

The Ninth Street newsstand carries the 10 out-of-town newspapers listed below. Help the customers find the newspaper they want by arranging them in alphabetical order by city.

Number the papers 1-10, then write the correct name across the top of each paper.

_____ The Pittsburgh *Press*

_____ The Cleveland *Plain Dealer*

_____ The Milwaukee *Journal*

_____ The Boston *Globe*

_____ The Atlanta *Constitution*

_____ The St. Louis *Post-Dispatch*

_____ The Washington *Post*

_____ *The New York Times*

_____ The Chicago *Tribune*

_____ The Los Angeles *Times*

# AUTHOR UNDER INVESTIGATION

Look up the word "author" in the dictionary.
Write the meaning in your own words. _____

_____

When we walk into a bookstore or a library and see rows and rows of books that we think we'd like to read, it is easy to forget that every single one of those books had to be written by a hardworking author. Sometimes an author has to work for a very long time before a book is finished.

1.  Write the name of one of your favorite books._____

2.  Write the full name of the author. _____

3.  Skim through the book and write a short paragraph to tell how old you think the author was and where you think he or she lived when the book was written.

    _____

    _____

    _____

4.  **Now do your research.**
    Ask your teacher or the librarian to help you find reference materials to "get the facts" about the author.
    Write a short paragraph to summarize your findings. _____

    _____

    _____

5.  Compare your 2 paragraphs. Were you

    _____ close to correct in your guess?
    _____ amazed at the difference?
    _____ surprised?

# A WORD OR TWO ON THE WORLD

You will need a world atlas or an encyclopedia to help you complete these geography lists.

1. Beginning with the letter **A**

an ocean _____

a continent _____

an island _____

a state or province _____

a major city _____

a desert _____

a mountain _____

2. One country beginning with each of the first dozen letters of the alphabet

A _____

B _____

C _____

D _____

E _____

F _____

G _____

H _____

I _____

J _____

K _____

L _____

3. A major river beginning with each of these letters

M _____

N _____

O _____

P _____

# CHOOSE A COUNTRY

Select 1 of the countries below. Use at least 3 different resources (books, magazines, pamphlets, encyclopedias, atlases, etc.) to find the correct information to finish the sentences.

* Thailand *          * Burma *          * Brazil *

_____
(name of country chosen)

1. Two countries that border this country are _____
_____ .

2. One of the most important industries of this country is _____ .

3. The capital city is _____ .

4. Two important cities located in this country are_____
and_____ .

5. Something that I found especially interesting about this country's

history is _____

_____

_____

_____

_____

6. A major holiday of this country is _____ . It is

celebrated by_____

_____

_____

# THE HUMBLE COOK

Ashriam is the best cook in all Elfland. He has served as chief chef for the great feasts of the most powerful kings, lords, and dukes in the land. In spite of this, he is a very humble elf. So humble, in fact, that when the Grand Duke asked him to prepare a list of his most famous dishes and their descriptions, it sounded too plain.

Use a thesaurus to help Ashriam find more colorful words to rewrite his descriptions.

**Partridge in a Pear Tree Pie:** chunks of meat and vegetables cooked together with special seasonings and baked into a pie

_____

_____

_____

**Ruby-Berry Sparkle:** ripe ruby-berries squeezed and strained and blended with spring water

_____

_____

_____

**Snowflake Cream Torte:** new snow mixed with cream and peach blossom nectar and churned until smooth and sweet

_____

_____

_____

# FINDERS KEEPERS

Find books in your library that feature each of the following well-known figures of folklore.

Write the full name of the book, the author, the publisher, and the date of publication beside each figure.

# LIBRARY LOVER'S LAW
## or
### The Ten Commandments for Library Lovers

♥ Thou shalt not speak above a whisper — of all the treasures of the library, silence is golden.

♥ Thou shalt remember to return or renew books and other materials <u>before</u> they are overdue.

♥ Thou shalt not fold, spindle, or mutilate any materials from the library. Treat books with care and respect — they belong to everyone.

♥ Thou shalt set out to learn where things are in the library. Knowing where to look is a valuable skill.

♥ Thou shalt not let too much time pass without visiting your library, for in the library you will discover many wonderful things.

♥ Thou shalt not reshelve books unless you know <u>exactly</u> where they go. A misshelved book is a lost book.

♥ Thou shalt not be afraid to report lost or damaged materials to the librarian. Nothing can be repaired or replaced if the librarian doesn't know about it.

♥ Thou shalt not forget to tell your friends about the good books you've read.

♥ Thou shalt seek to expand your interests and abilities by challenging yourself with good books.

♥ Thou shalt take much pride in your library. Use and care for what it has to offer.

# SKIMMING THE NEWS

Use information from a copy of your local newspaper to complete these sentences.

1. The front-page headline that most interests me is

   _____.

2. The name of the comic strip I like most is

   _____.

3. My horoscope for the day indicates that I should expect

   _____

   _____.

4. The weather forecast for tomorrow leads me to believe that I should wear

   _____.

5. A product that is advertised in the paper that I would like to own is

   _____.

6. The product is advertised by this company:

   _____

   and sells for this price: _____.

# RUNNING ERRANDS

Chris was given a list of errands to run.

Using the map below, write the number of the errand in the correct place where that errand will be done. Be sure to follow the direction arrows. The first one is done for you.

## List

1. Lock the door of the house as you leave (southeast corner of 89th St. and 1st Ave.).
2. Go to newsstand and buy today's paper (west side of 1st Ave. between 86th and 87th streets).
3. Pick up shoes at shoe repair (southwest corner of 87th St. and 1st Ave., next door to newsstand).
4. Buy a tube of toothpaste at the drugstore (northeast corner of 87th St. and 2nd Ave.).
5. Stop by the laundry and ask how late they'll be open (northwest corner of 87th St. and 1st Ave.).
6. Go to bakery and have a treat (east side of 1st Ave. between 87th and 88th streets).
7. Stop at fruit stand and buy a basketful of strawberries (southwest corner of 89th St. and 1st Ave.).
8. Take paper, shoes, toothpaste, and strawberries back home (southeast corner of 89th St. and 1st Ave.).
9. Surprise! I'll treat you to a movie! Meet me at the theater at 3:00 p.m. (southeast corner of 86th St. and 1st Ave.).

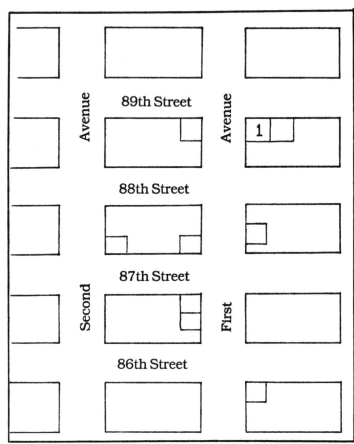

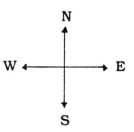

# READING PROJECT PLAN

Project Topic: _____

What I need to know: _____

Reading materials I will use: _____

**Project Plan**

Time: _____

Gathering and organizing information: _____

Activities: _____

Presenting project: _____

Evaluating completed project: _____

# WEIGHING AN ELEPHANT

Read the story below and supply the missing punctuation. Cross off each punctuation mark shown here as you use it.

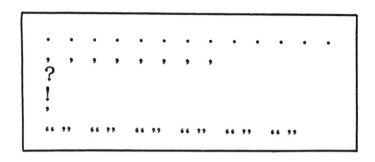

Many    many years ago a Chinese emperor was given an elephant by one of his loyal subjects    Being a very curious emperor    he immediately summoned his ministers

How much does this elephant weigh    he demanded

We do not know    the ministers replied    There are no scales large enough to weigh an elephant

A boy named Prince Chung had an idea    I can weigh the elephant    he announced calmly

Prince Chung led the elephant to a lake and placed the large animal in a boat    Then he got into the water and painted a line on the boat just above the level of the water

The elephant was removed    and the boat was filled with stones until it sank to the painted line    Then the stones were taken out and weighed    When the weights of all the stones were added together Prince Chung knew the elephant    s weight

You are very wise    Prince Chung    the grateful emperor said From now on you will be my respected friend

# OUTLINE PIN-UP

1. Write the name of a topic of interest to you on the pin-up line.
2. Think about what you want to know about this topic.
   Label each section of the line with one of the main ideas you want to know about. (Example: Ireland — folklore; history; people)
3. Fill each section of the line with information from reference books that fits into that section.

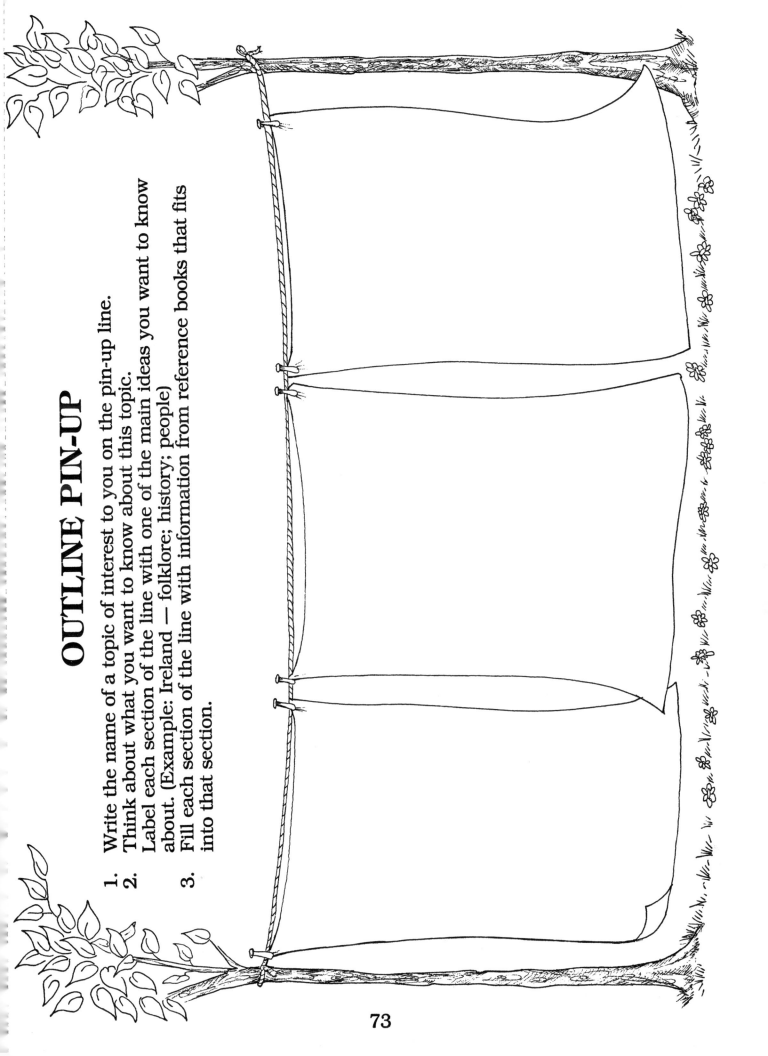

# RIDE THE UNICORN!

If you could really summon a magic unicorn by opening a book, and you and the unicorn could actually "ride into" the story, what book would you choose? _____

Why? _____

_____

_____

How would your presence change the story as you know it? _____

_____

_____

Name 3 other books you have read which you would have liked to be an actual part of. _____

_____

_____

Name 1 book whose story you would <u>never</u> want to enter. _____

_____

# CHARACTER SELECTION

Check a fairy tale book out of the library.
If you don't have a favorite, try one of these.

1. Douglas, Kate, ed. <u>The Fairy Ring</u>. New York: Doubleday & Company, Inc., 1967.
2. LeGallienne, Eva, trans. <u>Seven Tales by Hans Christian Andersen</u>. New York: Harper Brothers, 1959.
3. Lucas, Mrs. E. V., Lucy Crane, Marian Edwards, trans. <u>Grimms' Fairy Tales</u> by the Brothers Grimm. New York: Grossett & Dunlap, 1945.

Thumb through the book to find some fairy tales you would like to read.

Then find fairy tale characters in the stories to complete the sentences below.

1. I would nominate _____ for the "best personality" award

   because _____ .

2. I would like to spend a lazy Saturday afternoon with _____

   because _____ .

3. The character I would like to trade places with for a day is _____

   _____ because I could _____

   _____ .

4. I think it would be fun to have _____ come

   to our next school party if _____

   _____ .

The Fairy Ring
by Kate Douglas

# FAIRY TALE FAVORITE

The name of my favorite fairy tale is " _____

_____ ."

This story is about _____

_____

_____

_____

The most interesting character in the story is _____

because _____

_____

_____

I like this fairy tale better than the others I have read because _____

_____

_____

_____

_____

_____

_____

_____

_____

_____

# SHELVE IT!

Carefully read the list of book titles below. Then follow the directions and write the title of each book on its proper shelf.

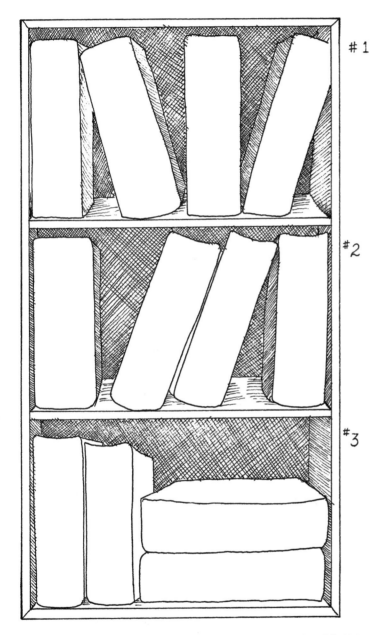

Titles

David Copperfield

The Elementary School Kids' Book of Lists

A Wrinkle in Time

The Yellow Pages for Students and Teachers

Roget's International Thesaurus

Dictionary of American Slang

Webster's Dictionary

Grimms' Fairy Tales

Mainly Math

The Hobbit

Gardening for Young People

Oceans and Continents in Motion

1. On the blank books on shelf #1, write the titles of all the books you would read for enjoyment.
2. On shelf #2, write the titles of those books that would help you with your schoolwork.
3. On shelf #3, write the titles of the books you would use to find information on a specific topic.

# GOOD BOOKS BELONG OUTDOORS

Here are a few suggestions for taking some of our favorite books outdoors!

- Find a stretch of sidewalk to sit on and share <u>Where the Sidewalk Ends</u> by Shel Silverstein with a friend who likes to giggle.

- Curl up under the shade of a leafy tree to enjoy <u>Charlotte's Web</u> by E. B. White.

- Tuck a copy of <u>If I Were in Charge of the World</u> (poems for children and their parents) by Judith Viorst in the family picnic basket.

- Bag a lunch, wear quiet shoes, grab your binoculars, hang on to <u>Birds</u> (from the <u>Golden Guide to Nature</u> series), and head out for an afternoon of bird-watching.

- Spend an afternoon making kites, painting with water, catching shadows or trying any number of other wonderful outdoor projects with the no-fail directions you'll find in <u>I Can Make a Rainbow</u> by Marjorie Frank.

- Save <u>The Sierra Club Summer Book</u> by Linda Allison for the hottest two weeks of the summer.

- Take a flashlight, a very special grown-up friend and <u>The Night Sky Book</u> by Jamie Jobb outside on the next clear night.

- On your next hike, pack some of the four tiny <u>Nutshell Library</u> books by Maurice Sendak in your knapsack or backpack. You'll be able to enjoy them at rest time.

- Stretch out on your stomach beside a stream or pond one lazy spring day with <u>The Adventures of Huckleberry Finn</u> or <u>The Adventures of Tom Sawyer</u> by Mark Twain.

- <u>On City Streets</u> by Nancy Larrick (poems about the sights and sounds and people of the city) is just right for reading or memorizing as you pause to people-watch on a busy sidewalk.

- Do yoga under the open sky with help from Rachel Carr's <u>Be a Frog, a Bird, or a Tree</u>.

- Read <u>In Granny's Garden</u> by Sarah Harrison and Mike Wilks before you begin the search for your own enchanted garden.

- <u>The Guinness Book of World Records</u> makes exciting treehouse reading. Then you'll want to get down from the tree and set some of your own records.

- When you've had the very worst day of your life, take <u>Alexander and the Terrible, Horrible, No Good, Very Bad Day</u> by Judith Viorst and go for a walk all by yourself!

## WERNER AND VICTOR — 34

An oxymoron is a combination of words that seem to contradict each other, such as laughing unhappily. Find and underline the 9 oxymorons in this story.

One day, Werner the wise fool and Victor the valiant coward decided to visit the city of Niccoo. As they followed their road through a dark forest, Victor asked Werner to take the lead so he could guard the rear. Werner though Victor should go first, as his bright sword would frighten away any thieves, but present fears are less than horrible imaginings! Victor said, "Yes, but the woods are far too dangerous for us." And he began to push with all his strength.

They walked on quickly through the forest. Suddenly Werner halted. They had come to the river, and the bridge was out! Ever the happy pessimist, Victor sat down and began to wail. "We'll never cross this river! We're stuck here." "Here is the solution, hiding in plain sight. We'll just push this tree over, and it will make a bridge across the river," said Werner.

Just then, a tiny giant appeared in a pool of black sunshine. In a voice like quiet thunder, he rumbled, "Who are you and why do you chop on my tree?" Victor jumped up and pushed him aside. "I'll chop the tree down with my sword!" he said, and began to chop with his bright blade. Victor's shaking knees gave way, and he fell to the ground. Werner quickly explained their problem, and begged the giant for help. But the two trembling travelers look so funny that the giant laughed and laughed until happy tears filled his eyes. By mistake, he bumped into the very tree that Victor had been chopping on, and it fell right over the river! Werner grabbed Victor and dragged him over the tree bridge, and they both ran until the laughing giant was far behind and they were out of the forest. Soon they could see the city of Nicoo just down the road. They were safe at last!

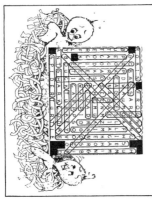

## WHAT'S THE WEATHER? — 17

Find and circle 30 compound words in the cloud. Words have been hidden horizontally, vertically, and diagonally, but never backwards.

The leftover letters from the puzzle spell a weather message. Figure it out and write it here.

_Whether the weather is told or whether the weather whether we like it or not._

## MIDNIGHT MADNESS — 36

Make this story more exciting by substituting a word from the list below for each underlined word. Use each word only once.

It was a dark, stormy night in Metropolis. The city lights shone wickedly in the wet streets, and the only night sounds to be heard were the crying of police cars and the howling of ambulances.

A rickety bus plodded around a corner and stopped in front of a dilapidated building. The neon sign above the door was blinking on and off in the night. Th... City H (d)... Full trash cans lined the hotel sidewalk, their tops fell to the ground with harsh noises as wandering cats and dogs squeaked through the trash.

As she sat on the bus, Joyce stared tiredly out the window at the sad scene with a falling heart. "I don't want to stay here," she moaned. "This hotel is old and shabby, and I'll bet it's dirty inside. It doesn't matter that our whole bunch will be collected. This area looks unsafe to me. I question whether our guide has stayed here previously before. Surely not! This place is just awful!"

Words to use: dreary; impetuous; glittered; wicked; run-washed; concrete; edged; crashes; stray; rubbish; OverFlowing; wander; vile

## SCRAMBLED EGGS — 20

Find and circle the names of 36 animals that lay eggs. The names go up and down, across, or on a slant, but never backwards or upside down.

The leftover letters spell the name of an egg-laying animal that roamed the earth long ago, but is now extinct.

Write the name of the animal that the leftover letters spell.

_dinosaur_

How many scrambled-egg breakfasts do you think just 1 of that animal's eggs would make?

## THE KNIGHT'S JOURNEY — 44

Read the story. Underline the topic sentence in each paragraph.

The Silver Knight sat astride his faithful steed, his polished armor glinting in the early morning sun. Both the knight and his mount were ready for His Royal Majesty, King Peter the Peaceful. The message he carried was to be delivered to the King of Tarm, for it was an invitation for the king and all his lords and ladies to attend a feast in celebration of ten years of peace between the two lands. By noon the Silver Knight had crossed the border into Tarm, and was trying to decide which of the unfamiliar roads would lead him to his destination — the Great Hall of Tarm.

Suddenly he heard someone approaching on horseback. He closed his visor, raised his shield, and made ready to draw his sword. Although there was peace between the two countries, the Silver Knight knew there were many other dangers, such as thieves and cruel highwaymen. Quietly guiding his horse off the pathway to the cover of a great old oak tree, the knight waited anxiously to discover the identity of the approaching rider.

Into the clearing before him emerged a splendid white horse, fitted with a halter of ostrich plumes and an apparent messenger. What could this rider be? The Silver Knight could tell from the horse's fittings and the knight's own shield that this was the king's own messenger intending to deliver a message to his own Great Hall of Tarm. The Silver Knight realized his mission, urged his horse forward into the clearing and approached the Knight of Tarm with a smile and a palm upraised in a token of peace.

## PIXIE POWER — 26

Fill each blank below with the best descriptive word from the list. Use each word only once.

Words to use:
cunning, marvelous, lonely, desolate, ruthless, horrifying, flaming, unsuspecting, fastidious, superstitious, evil, pudgy, eerie, mischievous, unfortunate

1. Pixies are believed to be tiny, _evil_ fairies who have _flaming_ red hair, pointed ears, and turned-up noses.

2. Legend has it that pixies love to mislead _unsuspecting_ travelers by causing them to become _bewildered_ and _confused_.

3. _Unfortunate_ travelers tricked by pixies can escape by turning their clothes inside out, as pixies are very _fastidious_ about dress.

4. Being trapped by pixies would be a _horrifying_ experience for a _lonely_ traveler on a dark and _desolate_ road.

5. Pixies are also accused of being _ruthless_ and _cunning_ horse thieves.

6. Some _superstitious_ people nail iron horseshoes above their barn doors to keep the _mischievous_ pixies away.

7. Even so, wouldn't it be a _marvelous_ experience to meet a pixie in all its _eerie_ splendor?

*Adventure lasts a lifetime if*
*You're willing to pursue*
*Each newly opened book to bring*
*The Unicorn to you!*